Take a Moment

Paul Christelis

Alex Hoskins

50
Mindfulness
Activities for Kids

MAYO CLINIC PRESS KIDS

MAYO CLINIC PRESS KIDS
An Imprint of Mayo Clinic Press
200 First St. SW
Rochester, MN 55905

mcpress.mayoclinic.org

To stay informed about Mayo Clinic Press, please subscribe to our free e-newsletter at mcpress. mayoclinic.org or follow us on social media.

For bulk sales contact Mayo Clinic at SpecialSalesMayoBooks@mayo.edu.

Proceeds from the sale of every book benefit important medical research and education at Mayo Clinic.

First American Edition 2024

ISBN: 979-8-88770-158-5 (hardcover)
979-8-88770-161-5 (ebook)

Library of Congress Cataloging-in-Publication Data is available upon request.

MANUFACTURED IN CHINA

SAFETY MESSAGE
Please supervise and help your child as necessary. Any physical activity has a risk of injury and all children have different abilities. Keep an eye on children to ensure that they do not force or strain too much. The exercises are not a subsitute for medical advice.

Contents

Hello! Welcome to TAKE A MOMENT, your very own guide to mindfulness.

You might not know what mindfulness is or how it can help you, so let's find out before we dive in and try the fun activities in this book.

Mindfulness is quite simple, really. It means taking notice of what is happening right now, in this moment.

There are many things you could be noticing. You might notice how your body is feeling, or if you are feeling a certain emotion. Or you could pay attention to what is going on around you—sounds, smells, or sights.

Being mindful also means that we are being friendly and curious toward whatever we notice—even unpleasant things, such as feeling stressed, worried, tired or upset.

Perhaps that sounds strange! "How can I feel friendly toward a worried feeling?" you might ask.

Well, in these mindfulness activities, we will find out how to welcome all experiences, even unpleasant ones, with an interested, friendly attitude.

We will discover how taking notice of our experiences in this way can help us to feel calmer, happier, and more confident.

Mindfulness can also help us appreciate the good things we have in our lives. For example, by choosing to notice the kindness of people around us we can feel happier and more grateful.

When we are really paying attention to the world around us, we discover things that are often hidden from our awareness! Even an activity as simple as walking barefoot on different surfaces can be full of sensations and make walking so much more interesting and eventful.

So now let's begin to take a moment and mindfully explore yourself and the world around you!

1

Mindful Breath and Body

This section includes activities that focus on breathing and body awareness. The breath and body are good "objects" to pay attention to because they are always available, wherever we are.

Mindfulness of breath and body activities have existed for thousands of years and have been known to help focus the mind and calm anxiety.

So, get ready to "listen" to what your body is telling you. If you listen deeply and with patience, you might find that you are able to feel more relaxed, calm, and confident, especially in any difficult or upsetting situations.

1. Breathing Hands

Sit comfortably and close your eyes.

Bring one hand up close to your nose, but without touching it. Feel your breath against your hand. How does it feel? Warm? Cool? Soft or strong? Like a breeze or a dragon's snort? There is no right or wrong way to breathe—everyone breathes in their own way.

Do this for one minute. If you feel your mind is wandering away from paying attention to your breath, then gently bring your attention back to the feeling of the breath on your hand.

When the time is up, see how many words you can think of to describe the sensations you felt on your hand.

2. Bellyful of Breath

You can do this activity sitting up or lying down.

Close your eyes and place one hand gently on your belly, so that the palm of your hand is covering your belly button. Let your attention go all the way into your hand. Breathe normally. Can you feel your hand moving with the belly? Maybe you feel your belly fill up as you breathe air into your lungs with the in breath? Can you feel your belly push out as you let go of the air on the out breath?

For the next minute or two, see what it's like to keep your attention on the feeling of your hand on your belly.

Do this activity if you want to feel calm and stop thinking about worries.

3. Tall as a Tree

You'll need a little imagination for this one.

Stand with your arms resting at your sides. You can keep your eyes open or closed. Now imagine that you have roots growing from under your feet, deep into the ground, just like the roots of a tree. What does that feel like? Maybe your legs feel sturdy and strong?

Imagine that your spine is the trunk of the tree growing upwards, and that the crown of your head is the very top of the tree. Perhaps there is the feeling of a gentle stretch all the way through your body.

See if you can stay in this position for a minute, breathing in and out.

4. Hug and Hop

**Give yourself
a friendly, loving hug.**

Wrap your arms around yourself, give a little squeeze and see if you can notice what that feels like. Let go and let your arms come back to your sides.

How does your body feel after the hug? Tingly? Warm? Something else?

Now, hop on the spot, as high as you like, about ten times. Stop hopping and stand still, noticing how your body feels now.

What's your breathing like? Give yourself a good ten seconds to notice this. Then, hug yourself again and pay attention to how that feels.

Continue moving between hugging and hopping for about a minute, noticing as many sensations in your body as possible.

5. Face Scrunch

In this activity, we are going on an adventure to a most interesting place—your face!

Close your eyes. Let's begin by paying attention to how the forehead is feeling. It's okay if you don't feel anything. Then try to notice your eyes and the space in between the eyes. Now notice your nose, your mouth (inside and out), your jaw, your cheeks, and your ears.

Next, see if you can scrunch up your face as much as possible and hold the scrunch for about five seconds. Let go of scrunching and notice how it feels for your face to go soft again.

Repeat the scrunch if you'd like, being sure to take time to notice all the sensations in your face.

6. Big Toe Boogie

How often do you notice how your toes are feeling?

Probably only if they are hurting! Your toes work so hard for you, wouldn't it be nice to give them a little friendly attention in return? Let's do that now.

While sitting or standing, take your attention all the way into the big toe of one foot. Without moving your toe, see if you can feel any sensations in it. Warmth? Numbness? Itchiness? Nothing? Don't rush this, even if nothing seems to be happening.

Then wriggle it around for a bit. Stop after a few seconds and notice what sensations are with the other big toe. If you'd like, why not try noticing all your toes? They will thank you for taking them out for a dance!

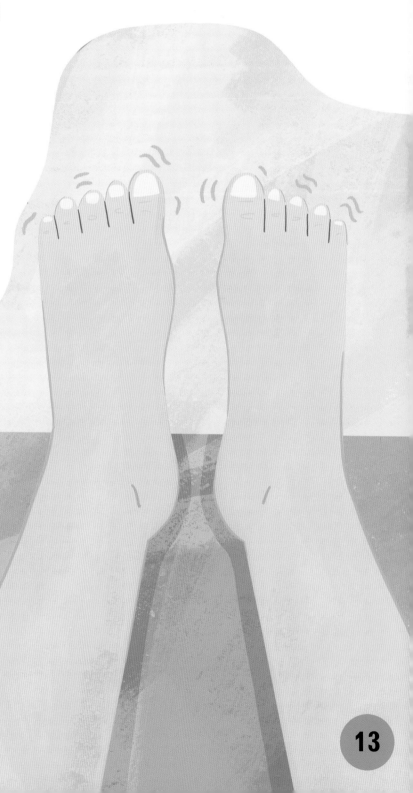

7. Still as Phil

Can you sit as still as Phil the cat?

Phil can sit still for ages, waiting for his lunch or for a treat, without moving a muscle! Can you sit as still as Phil?

Let's try. Sit comfortably and close your eyes. Notice the feeling of your breath moving. For the next minute, try to hold this still position even if you feel like moving.

Notice the feeling of wanting to move—to scratch an itch or rub your knee. Maybe you notice plenty of sensations in your body, maybe nothing at all.

Maybe, like Phil, you might open your eyes to find that lunch has arrived!

PHIL

8. Use 7-11 Breathing

This activity is especially helpful if you are feeling a bit nervous, upset or worried about something.

Sit comfortably and close your eyes. Breathe in to the count of 7 (counting silently to yourself), letting your in breath start at 1 and end at 7. Then pause. Now, breathe out to the count of 11. This will make your *out* breath longer than your *in* breath.

It may take a few practice rounds to get the length of the breath to fit the count. Keep breathing in this way for about two minutes, then open your eyes. How do you feel?

Using 7-11 breathing can make us feel calmer. It's like drinking a soothing hot chocolate to warm us up when we've been out in the cold!

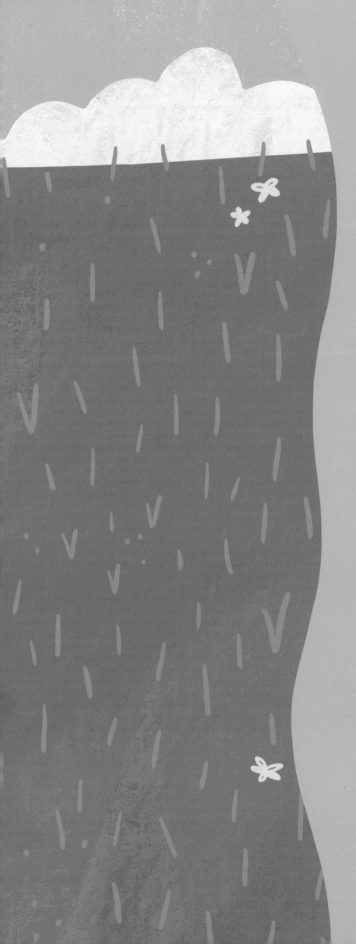

9. Body Ball

Get ready to be a ball!

Lie down on your side or back, on a comfortable surface (grassy lawn or carpet, maybe) and take a moment to feel your body resting on the ground. See if you can completely relax into the ground, like a marshmallow melting into a hot drink.

Now, bring your knees toward your chest and wrap your arms around your legs. Notice how that feels. What sensations do you feel in your body as you squeeze your knees into your chest?

If you'd like, rock your body gently from side to side, imagining that you have become a big ball. Ask yourself how your back feels, your neck, your legs. What other parts of your body do you notice? Do this for about a minute and then un-ball yourself.

Notice the feeling of stretching your body out again as you come to rest flat on the ground.

10. Bedtime Sighs

This activity is great for helping you get a good night's sleep.

Once you're comfortable in bed, close your eyes. See if you can remember something from the day that made you feel good or happy. As you remember it, breathe in deeply, imagining that you are breathing the good memory all the way into your body. Do this for five breaths. With each in breath you fill your body with the happy memory.

Take in one more deep breath, pause, and then breathe out any worries or unpleasant feelings that might be sitting inside of you. You can breathe them out with a big SIGH. Do this a few times, letting more worries flow out of you.

You should notice that your worries have disappeared into the air.

Think about your good memories and you'll soon have sweet dreams.

2

Mindful Looking and Listening

Our senses are always working, being pulled in so many directions at once! Because there is so much going on, our brains can take in only a tiny bit of this sensory information. The activities in this section and in Section 3 will help us to notice so much more than we usually do.

Using our senses to closely notice the world around us also has another benefit: it helps us to take a break from being in our heads and our thoughts. Too much time spent thinking can lead to worries or upset feelings, especially if our thoughts are about past events or concerns about the future.

So, do you know what silence sounds like? Have you stopped to really notice your hands? Get ready to find out...

11. The World in Your Hands

Have you ever stopped to really notice your hands?

No? Get ready for a surprise. Bring one hand close enough to your face so that you can see it clearly. Without rushing, take time to notice its shape and its color. Imagine that this is the very first time you have seen a hand!

Turn your palm toward you and inspect all the markings on the skin—lines, patterns, birthmarks. What about your fingers, nails, and fingerprints? How would you describe your hand to a creature from another planet who has no idea what a hand is or looks like?

Try your other hand now— is it the same as the first hand or can you spot any differences?

TIP: At first you might not notice anything interesting. Be patient though! And curious. You will discover details in your hands that you may have never noticed before!

12. Window Watcher

Windows are more interesting than you might think.

Find a window you can look out of and stand or sit in front of it. Imagine that the window frame is the frame of a painting and that everything you see through the window is the painting itself— a painting that is alive with color and movement.

Take a few minutes to watch the painting, noticing the shapes, patterns, or objects. Is there light or darkness? Movement or stillness?

Try to see as much as possible. You might be surprised to find that the longer you look, the more you see. Details are everywhere if we only have enough patience to spot them.

After three minutes of looking, write down as many details as you can remember.

13. Treasure Hunt

Treasures are easy to find.

Next time you are outside, (maybe in a yard or park) try to see how many things you can spot. These can be big (a merry-go-round) or tiny (a dewdrop on a blade of grass). All the things you spot are treasures.

After 10 minutes of looking, write down everything you saw. What was the biggest thing you saw? What was the smallest, the funniest, or the most beautiful? Treasures can be found anywhere if you just stop and look.

25

14. Flower Power

**Find a flower or
an interesting leaf.**

Imagine your eyes are so powerful that anything they look at becomes the most interesting thing in the world. Right now, this flower or leaf is full of incredibly interesting details. There is nothing else like it!

Take two minutes to look deeply into it and see how many small details you notice, such as shades of color, shapes, or markings on the petals. What does the flower or leaf feel like on your hand or between your fingers? Smooth? Hairy? Rough? How does it smell?

Don't rush! The longer you look, the more you'll see.

15. Mirror, Mirror

Everyone is different and unique.

When you look into a mirror, you will see someone who is unlike anyone else in the world. That's a marvelous thing! Take some time right now to notice what's unique about you.

Look at your reflection in a mirror and see if you can focus on every part of your face, one thing at a time. Start with your hair, forehead, then eyes, nose, mouth, and ears. Try to be curious about every body part and, as you take notice, imagine that you are making friends with that part of yourself. You could say—silently to yourself or out loud— "Hello eyes! Nice to meet you!"

It may feel a little strange at first but being friendly to your face can feel really great once you get the hang of it!

16. Hungry Ears

Imagine that your ears are hungry for sounds!

Sit with eyes closed and take your attention into your ears. For the next minute try to notice as many different sounds as possible. Some might be loud, others soft; some close by and others farther away. All sounds are welcome!

When you listen carefully, you are feeding your ears with delicious sounds. Even if you are in a quiet place, if you pay close enough attention, you will probably hear many different sounds floating around. Try it and give your ears a good meal!

TIP: Try to allow all sounds into your ears, even the ones that are unpleasant, such as a loud bang. And if there is only silence, enjoy that, too.

17. Sound Jar

You are going out on an expedition—to collect as many sounds as possible!

Go outdoors with a notebook and pen and set a timer for two minutes. When the timer starts, start listening. Every sound you hear goes into your imaginary sound jar. Write the sound down on a piece of paper and then listen for the next one.

What do you hear? Traffic? Leaves rustling? Dogs barking? Footsteps? When the two minutes are over, count all the sounds. If you are in a group of friends, see who was able to hear the most. Whose "jar" is the fullest?

TIP: If you'd like, why not use a real container? Maybe an empty jar or cookie tin?

18. Mystery Music

This is an activity for you and a partner.

One of you wears a blindfold while the other one collects a few objects. These could be anything: cups, bells, leaves, teabags...anything that makes a sound when rubbed between the fingers or against another object.

The blindfolded partner listens while the Mystery Maker makes sounds with one or more objects. Can the listener name all the different objects that are making the sounds?

You can be really creative: rub a dry leaf between your fingers; pour rice into a cup; tear a piece of paper in half...all these sounds are a special kind of mystery music. Then, swap places and let the Listener be the Mystery Maker, using a new set of objects.

19. Hummingbirds

You will need a partner for this activity.

Take turns being the Hummer and the Hearer. First, the Hummer hums a tune, any tune, into the Hearer's ear. Not too loudly, but loud enough that the Hearer can hear without difficulty.

After about 30 seconds, the Hummer stops and the Hearer then says what he or she heard. Try to describe what the hum sounded like: soft? smooth? rumbly? Or maybe high-pitched like a whistle? Be as descriptive as you can be.

Then swap! No two Hummers are the same: how were your hums different?

20. Silent Symphony

Get ready to make a silent discovery!

Have you ever noticed that silence isn't really silent? If you really listen, you will hear a lot of sounds in silence. Let's try it.

Find a quiet spot: maybe your bedroom or bathroom, go to a library, or you could put on headphones if you have them. Then close your eyes and for the next minute or two see if you can tune in to the silence around you.

At first you might not hear anything but be patient. Can you hear a rumbling? Buzzing? Maybe a sound you have never heard before! You might hear many different "instruments" playing in the orchestra of silence. All it takes is a little curiosity and patience.

TIP: Imagine, as you are listening, that your ears are growing larger and more powerful with every second of silence.

33

3

Mindful Tasting and Touching

When we pay attention, we notice so much more. Our tastes become fuller and our touches more sensitive. Everyday experiences, such as walking on grass or noticing how our clothes feel against our skin, become fresh and alive with detail.

We can learn to notice so much more than we usually do. Our surroundings become more interesting when we are curious about them: sounds are sharper, sights are more colorful, tastes are fuller.

Does a berry taste different if you eat it really slowly? How does a warm bath really feel?

Get ready to find out...

21. Sit for a Bit

How does it feel to sit?

This is something we don't really notice because our attention is often somewhere else. So, let's find out. Sit in a chair and close your eyes. If your feet are on the ground, notice the feeling of them making contact with the floor. You might also notice how they feel in your shoes or socks, if you are wearing any, or bare feet.

Then, move your attention to the places where your body is touching the seat: the back of your legs, or your back. What's that feeling of touch like? Warm? Cool? Comfortable or uncomfortable?

See if you can feel your full weight resting on the seat. Do you feel heavy or light or somewhere in-between? Finally, stand up. How does this feel different to sitting? Try this activity in different types of seats, such as dining table chairs or the sofa.

22. Meet the Air

Are you ready to get to know the air?

Stand or sit somewhere (a yard or park would be a good place) and begin to notice the feeling of the air against your skin. If the weather is warm, you might feel the heat of the sun, or if it's winter maybe there's a slight sting of cold. All of these sensations on the skin are like little greetings from the air.

The air may feel nice and friendly, or maybe a little uncomfortable (if it's a very hot or cold day). Try to relax for the next minute and allow yourself to befriend the air. After about a minute, notice if the air feels any different on your skin.

Tip: If it feels too uncomfortable, stop and go inside. The air should be a good friend!

23. Fast and Friendly Fingers

This simple activity takes just one minute.

Wherever you are, start exploring the space around you, using your fingers to touch and feel all the different surfaces you can find. *Be careful not to touch anything dangerous, such as a hot iron or oven!* Can you describe the sensation of each surface against your fingers? Some could be smooth, others rough, some cold, others warm…

Our fingertips have thousands of nerve endings in them, which means that they are able to feel more sensations than we can imagine. So, let your fingers go on an adventure and see how many different feelings you can discover.

24. Feeling Feet

Take your feet on an adventure to different lands.

You'll need to be barefoot for this activity. Begin in one room and walk around slowly, noticing the feeling of the floor on your feet. A woolly rug, hard wood, cool cement...each surface will feel different.

Then, once your feet have "tasted" enough of that surface, walk into another room or another part of the same room and give your feet a taste. Maybe this floor is colder, softer, or rougher? See how many different lands you can travel to, remembering to keep your attention in your feet as you travel.

TIP: If you do this outside, look out for any sharp objects and avoid them.

39

25. Water Wonderland

Try this fun activity the next time you have a bath.

Carefully put one foot into your bath. Really take time to notice the feeling of getting into the warm water. Pause, feeling the difference between your two feet. Then put the other foot in and notice how that feels.

Slowly lower your whole body into the water and feel the warmth spreading through you like a comfy blanket on your skin. If you have a bubble bath, feel the light, soapy bubbles with your fingers. What words can you think of to describe them? Maybe switch on the cold water and feel a jet of coolness wash over you.

When you are ready to get out, take some time to enjoy the sensation of drying yourself in a warm, cozy towel. How does your skin feel?

TIP: You can do the same with a shower, or getting into the pool, or the ocean!

26. Very Berry

Feel the flavor in this fun taste test.

Choose a berry you enjoy eating, such as a strawberry, raspberry, or blueberry. *(Ask an adult to make sure you're not allergic to berries.)* Now, instead of eating it really quickly, slow down and take at least one whole minute to chew, taste, and swallow the berry.

To start, put it in your mouth and feel it on your tongue. Before beginning to chew, roll it around in your mouth and notice how that feels. Maybe you feel the urge to bite, but be patient! When you do bite into it, pay attention to the explosion of flavor and then enjoy the feeling of chewing. Notice the feeling of swallowing. Now, see if you can describe what you noticed to a friend.

TIP: If you don't have berries, or are allergic to them, try another fruit or veggie instead.

27. Slow Breakfast

This activity can be done with the whole family, or with whoever is with you when you are eating breakfast.

Sometimes, we rush through our breakfast or do other things while we are eating, but in this activity everyone needs to agree to eat together, in silence, without distractions. It might seem a little strange at first, funny even, but give it a few minutes and see what you notice if you pay full attention to what you are eating.

Does your breakfast cereal make any sound when you pour milk over it? How gooey and sticky is peanut butter? What noise does peeling a banana make?

After a few minutes of silence, share your experience of what you heard, felt, or tasted with the others at the table.

28. First Food Fun

Get ready to experience the taste of something new!

Choose a food that you have never eaten before. (*Check with a parent or carer before you try a new food, in case you have an allergy.*) Slowly eat the piece of food, exploring its flavor and texture. Is it a pleasant taste, or an unpleasant one? Or maybe it is not really pleasant or unpleasant, just "okay."

After you have swallowed it, describe the taste to a partner. It doesn't matter if you liked the taste or not; what's important is that you are curious about trying something new and exploring the sensation of tasting something different. Now try something else new!

29. Sweet, Sour, or Something Else

Have fun with some new taste sensations!

Ask an adult to prepare a few different foods for you: some should be sweet, some sour, and some spicy, creamy, or something else.

Take a mouthful of each piece of food and slowly taste it. When you have swallowed it, say if the food was sweet, sour or something else. If it was something else, describe it as best you can. Maybe some foods are both sweet and sour, or a mixture of different flavors.

You can also be creative and try eating two or three foods at the same time (make sure they are small pieces!) Some flavors may go well together, others might taste strange! Find out for yourself.

TIP: Have a glass of water handy to rinse out your mouth after each taste. This will keep your tastebuds fresh.

45

30. Grateful Plateful

This is a great activity for the whole family.

Just before you are about to eat your meal, take a moment to notice every piece of food on your plate. Can you imagine the journey that each portion of food took to get to your plate? For example, your potatoes were bought from the store, which got them from the farmer, who planted them in the earth, which was nurtured by the sun and the rain...

Before you eat, be grateful for the journey each piece of food has made to get to your plate to feed you. Then, as you eat, really enjoy the wonderful flavors as the food continues on its journey—to your belly!

4

Mindful Emotions

Some emotions are pleasant to feel, such as happiness, while others can feel unpleasant, such as anger or sadness. Mindfulness helps us to feel and experience all emotions by learning to notice them in a friendly and curious way.

This doesn't mean that sad or angry feelings simply go away, but if we can notice those feelings and allow them to be what they are, they will often become less unpleasant to be with.

When we learn to observe our feelings, we begin to see that they are all constantly changing. We then realise that life is a big adventure with lots of different emotions, so we can enjoy the pleasant ones when they come along and not worry too much about the unpleasant ones because we know they won't last.

The activities in this section include opportunities to notice a wide range of emotions that you might feel in different situations. Many of them can be done in groups—it is helpful to notice how other kids experience emotions, too.

31. Welcome the Weather

You are invited to discover your "inner weather"!

Outside may be sunny or cloudy, rainy or dry, but what about the weather inside you? Have a look and see. Close your eyes and ask yourself "How am I feeling right now?" Then, wait a while as you "listen" to what your emotions are telling you.

Emotions are like the weather—sometimes pleasant, sometimes not. Are you feeling upset or angry like a storm, or peaceful and happy like a warm afternoon? Or something else? Whatever it is you are feeling, see if you can just let it be there. Even if it's an unpleasant feeling, it will change—just like the weather!

32. Emotion Explorer

Did you realize that when you feel an emotion, such as sadness or happiness, your body feels it, too?

The next time you feel an emotion, see if you can pause for a few moments, close your eyes, and ask yourself, "Where in my body do I feel this anger/worry/happiness /excitement?" Maybe your whole body feels it? Or perhaps the feeling is strongest in your chest, or your belly, or somewhere else?

We are all different and we experience emotions in our own ways. Once you have found where the emotion is, spend a little while noticing how it feels. Share what you have discovered with a parent or friend.

33. Moody Music

For this activity you and your friends or family will all need to choose a piece of music.

Take turns to play about a minute of a piece of music. It can be anything; something you like or don't like. Then, while the music is playing, notice how it makes you feel.

Some music lifts our mood up, makes us feel happy and light; some music can make us feel heavy or sad. There are all kinds of feelings that music can bring out of us.

After you have heard a minute of the music, switch it off and all share how it made you feel. You might be surprised that you don't all feel the same feelings! Then, play someone else's choice and listen again for how the music affects your mood.

34. Worry Truck

Use the Worry Truck to drive your worries away!

We all have worries from time to time—it's normal and natural. But sometimes, the worries can pile up and take up a lot of space inside our head. That's why it can help to have your own Worry Truck.

You can either make your own Worry Truck using cardboard and pens, or find an old box and draw a truck on it. Then, if there is something you are worried about, write the worry on a small piece of paper, fold it up and put it inside the Worry Truck. Do this every time a worry comes along (it could be the same one or a new one.)

At the end of the day, tip out all the worries into the trash and return. Now you don't need to worry about them overnight. Your truck is empty and ready for tomorrow's worries.

TIP: It also helps to talk to someone about your worries. Sharing worries makes them easier to cope with.

MY WORRY TRUCK!

35. Happy Movies

Make your own movie! The title of your movie is: WHAT MAKES ME HAPPY.

To begin making your movie, sit somewhere comfortable and close your eyes. Now, think of a time you felt really happy. Picture where you were, who was with you, what you were doing and how it felt. Watch this memory in your head for a couple of minutes, just as you might watch a movie on a big screen.

As you watch it, notice how your body is feeling. Where do you feel the happiness? In your chest? Your belly? Your toes? Let the movie play a few times over.

You could do this activity with a friend and take it in turns to tell each other about your movie.

TIP: You can also watch a Sad Movie, Angry Movie, Excited Movie—whatever movie you choose. While watching these it is helpful to remember that they are only movies and they will come to an end.

36. Rushing River

Use this activity to help you feel calm.

Sometimes, your mind feels too full and busy with thoughts and feelings, especially if you are upset about something. When this happens, invite yourself to pause for a minute and imagine that you are sitting comfortably on a riverbank.

Feel the warm grass beneath you and hear the sound of the river flowing past. Imagine that all of the upset thoughts and feelings inside you are leaves floating on the river. Now, watch the leaves being swept away down the river, all the way into the distance.

Maybe more upset feelings flow past...that's fine, because you are sitting still, watching. You watch as the leaves come and go, as the water continues to rush. Stay like this for a while, feeling the grass beneath you as your troubles float away.

37. Emotion Ocean

Let the ocean wash your worries away.

Just imagining the ocean can make us feel better. Try it now. Close your eyes and picture a big ocean. Can you hear the seagulls or the waves? Can you smell the sea salt?

Picture yourself standing on the shore holding a bottle in your hand. The bottle contains an unpleasant emotion you have felt recently. Maybe the label on the bottle says "JEALOUS" or "ANGRY." Now, see yourself tossing the bottle far into the sea and watch as it sinks all the way down to the ocean floor and disappears from sight. The big ocean now holds your unpleasant emotion so you don't have to worry about it any more.

38. Bliss Bath

This activity is a real treat!

Make yourself comfy, sitting or lying down, and close your eyes. Now, see if you can remember a time when you felt really happy or good. Picture yourself in the happy situation—maybe someone said something nice about you or you were having a fun time on vacation, etc.

Can you feel the good feeling in your body right now? A tingling or a warm glow perhaps? Whatever it is you feel, imagine that you are now getting into a bubble bath full of this good feeling. See yourself relaxing into the bubbly, happy water and see if you can really feel the goodness all over your body.

Every time you take a breath, you sink a little deeper into the water and your body soaks up more and more of the lovely feeling. Ah...bliss!

39. Emoji Party

You will need paper and pens for this fun activity.

Look at pictures of different emotion emojis. If you don't know what an emoji is, ask an adult to show you. Say what emotion the emoji is feeling. Now it's your turn to draw your own emoji. Choose an emotion you are feeling right now and draw an emoji of it. If you don't really feel anything now, think about a time you did feel an emotion and draw that.

If you do this activity with a friend or in class, you could all share your emojis and guess what the emotion is. All emojis are welcome at this party because we all feel these different emotions some of the time. They belong to all of us.

Tip: if you are not feeling anything you could also draw an emoji of "not feeling any-thing"! What kind of expression would that be?

A LITTLE...

A LITTLE
MORE...

A
LOT!

40. A Little, A Little More, A Lot!

It's fun to do this activity in a group, or you could also do it with just one friend.

Find a space in a room where you can move about. Your teacher or friend calls out an emotion, for example, ANGRY, and then invites you to feel three different amounts of it; a little, a little more, and a lot.

First, see if you can feel A LITTLE anger. Move around if you want to and let your body show what A LITTLE anger feels like.

Then, move on to A LITTLE MORE anger. Let your body express how that feels.

And then: A LOT of anger. What's your body doing now? Did you feel a difference each time the amount of anger went up? Where in your body did you feel it? Now, do the same for a few other emotions.

TIP: It's nice to end this activity with a pleasant emotion, such as LOVE or JOY.

HAPPY!

5

Mindful Appreciation

In this section, we are all invited to appreciate ourselves, the people we care for, and the world around us.

When we are thankful and kind toward ourselves and others, life feels so much better! We realize that there is so much to be grateful for, but to really notice this we need to stop and pay attention to it. If we are too distracted by thoughts about what happened yesterday, or about what might happen tomorrow, then we could miss all the good things that are happening right now!

So get ready to discover the many good things, big and small, happening with you and around you.

41. Good Morning!

This is an activity for the whole family and a great way to start the day!

Each morning, maybe when you are all having breakfast, take a moment to each complete the following sentence: "Good morning, World! Thank you for yesterday. The thing I appreciated most about yesterday was…" and then say what you most appreciated, for example, "I appreciated my yummy dinner" or "I appreciated when my friend helped me in class."

As you share what you appreciated, notice how your body feels as you share it. Where is the feeling of appreciation? In your chest? Belly? Somewhere else?

Then, see if you can pay attention to what happens today so that you can thank it tomorrow! Try this activity for a week and see how it makes you feel.

42. Find the Kind

For this activity, you will be a Kindness Detective, and your special mission is to "Find the Kind!"

Kindness is all around us but we often don't notice it. Starting at the beginning of your day, watch out for anything kind that is happening around you. It could be your pet giving you a friendly lick, or your teacher saying something nice to you. Or maybe a friend giving you one of their snacks...

At the end of the day, write down all the acts of kindness in a notepad. Do you have a favorite one? Share it with someone, such as your parent or sibling. You are now passing on the kindness! Can you find more kindness tomorrow? Can you give out some kindness, too?

GET WELL SOON.

I LOVE YOU, GRANNY.

I MISS YOU.

43. Share the Care

Share some caring thoughts.

Think of someone you know who is having a tough time—a sick relative, an unhappy friend, anyone who might be upset about something. Take a few moments to see this person in your thoughts. Can you feel what they might be feeling?

Then, imagine that you are sending them caring, friendly thoughts. Maybe these thoughts look like ribbons, or clouds, or you can choose what they look like. Imagine that these thoughts are floating away from you and finding their way to the person you are thinking about.

How does it feel to send these caring thoughts?

44. Happy Dreams

Do this activity last thing at night before you go to sleep.

On a piece of paper, write down three things that happened today that made you feel grateful or happy. They could be really small, such as "when the sun came out after the rain" or "the taste of chocolate."

Then, fold up the paper and place it inside your pillow. While you sleep, these three things will be close to your head and perhaps even find their way into your dreams!

The next morning, take the paper out of the pillow and put it in the recycling bin, where it can go to become fresh paper for more happy thoughts to be written on.

Things I am grateful for:

1. My favorite chocolate bar.

2. Playing soccer with my friends.

3. My favorite TV show.

45. Bestie Bubbles

You will need a bottle of bubbles and a bubble wand for this activity.

Close your eyes and think about all the people in your life that make you feel good: family members, friends, teachers. Really feel the good feelings in your body— maybe you feel tingling, or a big, warm feeling in your chest. Then, take a big breath full of these happy feelings and blow them into the bubble wand.

All the bubbles that stream out of the wand are full of your happy feelings!

Watch as the bubbles float away and pop into the air, spreading your good feelings all around.

Pause and start again. Do this as many times as you like. How many happy bubbles can you send out into the world?

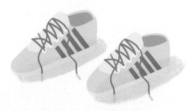

46. Thank you, body

Appreciate the body that you have.

When was the last time you thanked your body for all it does for you? Just think of everything it does for you during the day. It's time to send a little love to your body now to say "thank you!"

Close your eyes and begin by noticing how your feet are feeling. Then, silently say "Thank you, feet!" Move up your body slowly, saying "Thank you" to other parts: legs, arms, hands, tummy, head, heart...

Thank as many parts of you as you like. If there is a part of your body that is injured or hurting, you can give it a little extra attention and send it "Get well soon" wishes instead. After each thank-you, take a deep breath in and imagine that part of your body smiling back at you.

47. Three Good Things

This activity reminds us that, even when we are feeling down, there are things to feel good about.

Think of something that makes you feel disappointed, upset, sad, or worried. Then, imagine you have a special bucket and that you are putting this feeling in the bucket.

Now, think of three things that make you feel good, happy, or okay. Put these three feelings in the bucket too. Notice that the good feelings and the sad feelings can all be in the bucket at the same time. Maybe they are different colors? Do these colors mix to form a new color or do they stay separate?

From time to time you may want to tip the feelings out of your bucket and put new ones in. Or you can keep the old ones and keep filling the bucket anyway. There is always space for more!

48. Hello, Earth

If you've ever wanted to travel into space, this activity is for you!

Close your eyes and prepare to blast off into space. Imagine that you are far away from Earth. If you look down you can see our planet at a distance, a big round ball full of amazing natural wonders, from beautiful deep, blue oceans to the lush, green rainforests that are full of extraordinary creatures.

Take time from your peaceful spaceship to notice and appreciate as many things on Earth as possible. What do you see? For each thing you notice, see if you can quietly send your appreciation to it, from the biggest ocean to the smallest creature. We humans would not exist without all the wonders of nature around us.

Your space mission will bring you back home to Earth soon—just open your eyes when you're ready to return.

49. Dear Me...

Who is the person you spend most of your time with? The answer is easy: it's YOU, of course!

You spend 24 hours every day with yourself, so if you can be kind and friendly towards yourself, you will enjoy your own company a lot more! Write a short but honest letter (or postcard) to YOU, telling yourself all the things you like or appreciate about you.

Start by addressing it to "Dear Me," and then write as many kind things as possible. For example, "I like that I am helpful around the house and that I try hard at school." When you are finished, put your letter in an envelope and write your name and address on it. Ask your parent or carer for a stamp and mail using a mailbox away from home. Then, get ready to receive it and read it when it's posted back to you.

TIP: You could also write a postcard about things you would like to improve about yourself. For example, "I'd like to tidy my bedroom more often" or "I'd like to get better at soccer."

50. Stop Right Now!

This activity helps us to appreciate the small things that we often don't notice.

Whatever you are doing, wherever you are, stop right now and PAUSE. Take a moment to look around you. What do you see? Notice as much as possible. What do you hear? Listen carefully to all the sounds (or the silence.) Do you smell anything? Feel anything? Maybe an emotion or a sensation in your body? There is so much to notice right now.

Make this moment special by thanking it. Yes, even if it doesn't seem exciting, this moment right now will lead to the next one, and the next one, and who knows where that one will lead to? Each moment is an adventure into the next moment! So, thank this moment right now for being exactly as it is.

Notes for parents and caregivers

Mindfulness is a way of paying attention to our present moment experience with an attitude of kindness and curiosity. Most of the time, our attention is distracted—often by thoughts about the past or future—and this can make us feel anxious, worried, self-critical, and confused. By gently moving our focus from our busy minds and into the present moment, we begin to let go of distraction and learn to tap into the ever-present supply of joy and ease that resides in the here-and-now. Mindfulness can also help us to improve concentration, calm unpleasant emotions, and even boost our immune systems.

The mindfulness activities in this book can help your child be calmer, less anxious, more focused, and even more energized. The activities are appropriate for a wide range of situations, whether you're at home with your child, playing or walking outdoors, or even while you're on holiday. You may want to dip into the book at random and choose a few activities that suit the environment you're in, or perhaps you and your child will prefer to focus on a particular section of the book.

Although all the activities promote well-being through mindful awareness, some are particularly helpful for certain conditions. For example, if your child is having difficulty sleeping, the **Mindful Breath and Body** section would be a good source of support: focusing on body sensations and breathing helps to calm the nervous system and an overactive mind.

The sections on sensory awareness encourage curiosity, creativity, and attentiveness, and those activities that require a partner or group facilitate relational mindfulness and cooperation, which aids the development of empathy and social skills.

Don't sit back and watch your child do the activities. Join in! Not only will you benefit from a mindful break but you will almost certainly have fun and get to know your child better, too. Taking part in the activities will encourage your child to really engage with them. They also give you an opportunity to talk and spend more time with your child, and your child will feel more comfortable opening up about their experiences.

Notes for teachers

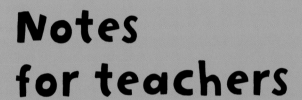

Most of these activities can be easily experienced in the classroom. You can either choose to have a regular Mindfulness Activity slot each day, at a set time, or spontaneously invite the class to participate in an activity when inspiration strikes!

Having a set time each day (first thing in the morning, for example) helps to embed mindfulness as a habit (the brain learns to anticipate the activity and thus cultivates the habit more effectively). For example, you may wish to encourage wakefulness after lunch so this would be the perfect opportunity for an activity such as **HUG AND HOP** or **FACE SCRUNCH**. If what's needed is calming down before a test, then **7-11 BREATHING** is your go-to activity to help regulate the nervous system.

Some activities will require a little planning: some classroom equipment perhaps, or asking children to bring an object from home.

Where possible, if weather permits, make use of the outdoors. This is a real antidote to the sedentary, digitally-bound lives we tend to lead.

Whatever activity you choose, be sure to spend sufficient time afterward sharing experiences, in pairs or small groups. Children will learn that we are all unique, sensory beings with our own responses to the world and that this variety should be celebrated. Indeed, this is one of the wonderful gifts of mindfulness: there is no right or wrong answer to what you experience, there is simply YOUR experience. And all experiences are welcome!

Glossary

allergy when someone's body reacts badly to eating or coming into contact with something in particular. The allergy may cause vomiting, a skin rash, swelling of the skin, sneezing, difficulty in breathing, or another reaction

anxiety feeling worried or nervous that something bad is going to happen

appreciation showing gratitude for somebody or something

attention taking notice of somebody or something by listening or watching carefully

birthmark a mark on the skin that has been there since you were born

confident feeling sure of your own ability to do something

cooperation working together to achieve the same aim or result

dewdrop a very small drop of water, one of many that form on the ground overnight

emotion a strong feeling, such as love, fear, or happiness

empathy being able to understand another person's feelings or experiences

feelings a person's emotions, such as anger, happiness, joy, or sadness, rather than their thoughts or ideas

habit something that you do often, without thinking about it

immune system the cells, body tissues, and body organs that work together to protect the body from infection.

nerve ending the end of one of the many long fibers that carry messages between the brain and all parts of the human body

nervous feeling afraid or worried about something

nervous system all the nerves (long fibers) that carry messages between the brain and all parts of the human body

nurture care for somebody or something while it/they are growing or developing

patience being willing to wait

rainforest thick forest, usually growing near the equator, where it rains very often

sedentary spending most of the time sitting down, or not moving around

sensation a feeling, or the ability to feel through touch

senses sight, hearing, smell, taste, and touch—the body's ways of getting information from the world around us

sensory information the information collected by our senses, and sent to the brain

stress worry or pressure caused by problems in someone's life

taste bud one of several small parts of the tongue that allow you to taste

unique the only one of its kind

Further information

BOOKS

Acorns to Great Oaks: Meditations for Children
by Marie Delanote
(Findhorn Press Ltd, 2017)

Anxiety Relief Workbook for Kids
by Agnes Selinger
(Rockridge Press, 2021)

Calm: Mindfulness for Kids
by Wynne Kinder
(DK Children, 2019)

Mindfulness and Me
by Katie Woolley and Rhianna Watts
(Mayo Clinic Press Kids, 2023)

Mindfulness and My Body
by Katie Woolley and Rhianna Watts
(Mayo Clinic Press Kids, 2023)

Mindful Me: Breath by Breath; Exploring Emotions; Get Outdoors; Sleep Easy: mindful stories for kids
by Paul Christelis
(Watts, 2018)

Peaceful Like a Panda
by Kira Willey
(Rodale Kids, 2020)

WEBSITES

www.bbcgoodfood.com/howto /guide/10-mindfulness-exercises-kids
10 more quick and simple mindfulness activities to do

www.kidshealth.org/en/kids /mindfulness.html
More information about what mindfulness is

https://mcpress.mayoclinic.org/parenting/
Expert parenting resources from the most trusted name in health

www.positivepsychology.com /mindfulness-for-kids
Some more mindfulness activities to try

Index